Anarchic Structure

Ayden Payne

BookLeaf Publishing

India | USA | UK

Presentation by *BookLeaf Publishing*

Web: www.bookleafpub.com

E-mail: info@bookleafpub.com

ISBN: 978-93-5744-333-3

First edition 2022

DEDICATION

Dedicated to my Dad, Jack Keet. You brought me up as your own and never failed to believe in me.

ACKNOWLEDGEMENT

I would like to acknowledge Charlee Munn for giving me the nudge to create this book. Chaz for always being there, helping me through the dark times and celebrating the good. Marge for always offering counsel and being a Hippo. Shannen for being the okayest big sister I could ask for and last but not least my Nan for being a second Mum to me and Shannen.

Roots

Back in my home town
Seen all the same clowns
Avoiding them like the plague
Keeping my intentions vague
To those I don't want to see
Trying to be a different me
It's harder than I imagined
Don't need the 30-day badge and
I'll keep doing it by myself
No need to look at the top shelf
Of the bar I work in
Life not heading to the bin
No longer feel like trash
Not waiting on the inevitable crash
Keeping the mind healthy
Avoiding the cretins, stealthy
Start college in September
Going to become a member
Of the life plan society
Let's get over that anxiety
Follow the path
And be sure to laugh
Find happiness in the small things
See what the road brings
The good and the bad

It's okay to feel sad
Make these words take you somewhere
People do care
About what you have to say
Stop worrying about the pay
It's all immaterial
Not living off dry cereal
Have a family that cares
Not about the wares
That I bring home

Only that I am me and home

Is The Grass Greener?

Corrugated metal roof,
The fortunate walk past aloof.
Luxuries are none,
Play with debris for "fun".
Water from a tap?
No way to afford that!
Broken shed...
Somewhere to rest an exhausted head.
Skyscrapers loom,
A sense of impending doom.
Stale loaf of bread,
Better than being dead?

We are the outcasts!
Long will we outlast.
"Cockroaches" on the earth,
Wishing for a greater girth!
Children cry,
The lame lie,
Unable to move...
Have they anything to prove?

We are the refugees!
Almost as famous as the fugees.
Sad songs to sing,
What will the wealthy bring?
Sympathy and clothes,
What about the circling crows?

Save us from this monstrosity!
Is this really the place to be?

"Leaders" of Britan

Leaders of Britain
You seem awfully smitten
With the oil barons of the east
Those who probably care the least
About this land
Yet you all band
Together like a swarm
Not bothered about the soldiers marching out at
dawn
Back alley trades
While police carry out raids
Making it seem like the evil is coming
Innocent children scared, running
Mythical wars
The same lies, it bores

When will you grow a spine
And stop reading out the same line
"Strong and stable"
More like weak and inable
Where is your plan?
I'm not sure you can
See past your own noses
You think your asses smell like roses
I've seen humbler people on the street

Barely affording shoes on their feet
Give up your salary for a year
Then it will all become clear
The only problem here
Is you.

Perception of The Streets

Soulless eyes,
As common as the household fly.
Dirty, tatty and worn.
Their life has been torn,
Apart by the cold nights.
Oh great another flashlight!
"Move along please."
The words glide with ease.

Mouldy blankets,
Let's give thanks it's
Summertime.
But nothing is fine,
Sleeping bags to lug around.
Been out of house since Gordon Brown.

Drugs and alcohol numb the pain,
Remember that guy Wayne?
Respectable man...
Seemed to be heading somewhere with a plan.
Now sits on the street,
With a simple sheet:
"Need money for food."
White collar class look ahead rude.
We are the faceless,

Live our lives traceless.

If an elite decides we should be removed...
Who else would have approved?

Man's Best-friend

They start off small and yappy
Yet they make most happy
Some grow to the size of a pony
Others could race in the grand prix
Head scratched never end
They'll drive you round the bend
Leaving presents on the carpet
Some lead sheep to market
Others are a ball of fluff
Every now and then they're a right scruff
Make you jump with a deep bark
Treated like a monarch
In some households
Easily obsessed with their many folds
They'll love you the most
Even if they chew up your post
Always a happy tail at the door
Would lick you sore
Indisputably man's best friend
They're for life not a trend

Bubble

We are coloured souls,
Wondering through this rocky world,
Hoping to achieve our goals,
The daily struggles,
Irrelevant to the select few,
Who often have tussles,
With the elite crew,
The motley bunch,
Those who invent words such as a the credit
crunch.

Our identity,
Masked by the obscenity,
Of the pig headed,
Often feeding us the dreaded,
Empty promises and lies,
As our uniqueness dies,
We become robots to the system,
Living in a ciste'n,
Of anarchy and hate,
The majority more fearful of being late,
Than looking beyond their bubble,
To the real world struggles.

Extremists and diseases,
Publicly displayed only when it pleases,
The elite few,
The motley crew,

Now I ask who are you?

Drugs

Don't experiment with drugs
Or you'll join the thugs
But you MUST have the vaccines
Or no club nights for the teens
No trial or test
But we know what's best
The whole world stopped
"normal" life dropped
For a better one?
The government is done
With pretending to care
Now people stop and glare
If you don't have a covering
Too many people still suffering
Living in a first world poverty
Is it Dinner or Tea?
No money for either
One big deceiver
Called Boris
An absolute Doris
Dithers and dathers
As the "extremists" gather
Illegal to protest
Stopping progress
1000's can join for football

And the inevitable brawl
But no live music
Silence the acoustic
Of the theatre
More money for the realtor
And the private landlords
While independents are putting up boards
The billionaires flourished
And the poor were more malnourished
Took a teenager to feed the young
And his praises are sung
Track and trace
Another control of your space
A phallic rocket from a tax dodger
Making up for his little todger
It's down to us to be responsible
Well that's impossible
No Vaccine for me
Just leave me be!

Smile

Writing about something happy
Often comes across as sappy
Words of love and beauty
Can be seen as snooty
It seems like in this world
It's easy to be whirled
Into the negative perspective
It's actually quite infective
But search for the good
And if you could
Spread some joy
Come now don't be coy
What is it that makes you smile?
Do you stare at the clouds for a while,
Or watch the dogs in the park?
The stars shining through the dark,
Or the innocence of a child?
Maybe running through the wild?
The smell of the forest
Or the colours of a florist?
Appreciating fine art?
Letting out a solid fart?
It's often the simple things we overlook
Like finishing a good book

That bring a light to our eyes
Be wise
To take the time
Listen to this Rhyme

And smile

Death Spoke to Jack

Death saw him getting tired, saw that he needed
rest
Saw that life was hanging heavy on his tight and
weary chest.
He knew that there was not a cure, Jack didn't
want to be a burden,
So Death held him close and spoke these words,
of this I am certain.

I'm sorry Jack but your time is here, I know it's
hard but have no fear
The family and friends you've left behind, in
their memories they'll always find
The lessons and love from the man that you
were. Time flies by in a blur

From kids to grandkids you've seen them grow,
all caught up in life's flow
You've nurtured and cared for all around. It's
time to rest now, don't make a sound.
Follow me now into the next place, In
everyone's hearts you hold a big space.

Jack took his last breath and closed his eyes,
knowing that Julie was by his side.
Death held Jacks life warm in his hands and it
was then that he knew the greatness of this man.

With tearful eyes we watched him suffer, saw
him slowly fade away,
And whilst we loved him fiercely, we could not
make him stay.
A golden heart stopped beating, hard working
hands put to rest.
Today we remember the life of a man who
simply was the best.

Every Cloud

People say every cloud
And to be fair I am quite proud
Of leaving the bar trade
For a job that see's me paid
To stand here and write
And no longer fight
With drunken bums
Acting as their mum's
Because they can't handle a drink
Gives me time to think
About what words to say
In a certain way
To get my point across
Can be my own boss
Just me here
As the OAP's peer
Through the glass
And continue to pass
Plodding along
To their own song
No music to be heard
Barely spoken a word

Does my voice still work?
Tasks I cannot shirk
Best get back at them
At least I don't cough up phlegm

The Walk Home

The innocence that's on your face
It just might be your saving grace
Walking home with keys in hand
Looking out for the band
Of dreaded hoods
Coming to take your goods
Darkened eyes watch you go
Glance around high and low
Watch the alleyway
Or you may be prey
Even police cannot be trusted
You still might be found grey and crusted
They'll band together
Like birds of a feather
Deny it all
And your name will fall
To the lost and forgotten
While your body isn't yet rotten
Be safe out there
I know it isn't fair
To have to be so aware
It is slowly changing
The abuse less ranging
If you ever find yourself lost
Know this man won't let you be crossed

Think Twice

What's that smell?
Is that a man?
Surely not, that's more grime than tan!
Ragged beard hides a face
That's seen so much
Life at a fast pace
A bin lid bangs
And takes him back
In his mind his sanity hangs
On by a thread
Overhead,
Is that birds or bombs?
Those people staring
A crackling through comms
Are they a threat or just a civi?
Palms do tingle
They miss the pistol
The cold comfort
Of a death machine
Quick find a tool
Protect your country
"on the ground!"
The voice in memory?
Cuffs go on
And back again

A cold, dark cell
Oh not again!

This man has seen too much
Holding on to a crutch
His leg has gone with his mind
When he trod on that mine
Think twice about this man
Is he crazy or a hero?

Or is he just ones and zeros?

Colour

What if I told you the sky was green?
Would you believe it having seen,
The colours it can glow?
Or if I was to show,
That the grass beside you luminated pink?
Would you question what you had to drink?
Now imagine a world where there was no colour
Would that not be a bummer?
Blacks to whites is all to see
Maybe a grey to give you glee
This is the world some do live
Their perception different
Some people ignorant
That colours are not just one thing
But a beauty to our eyes they bring

The Hunt

Peering under benches
Hoping as your jaw clenches
To find the discarded ends
Not choosy about the blends
Of leaf within the paper
Just craving that blueish vapor
Black can clutched tight
"excuse me mate, got a light?"
Deep intake to kill the craving
Down 'til there's nothing left for saving
Stained fingers groping
While tired eyes are scoping
For the next hit
Out with the black specked spit
A quarter of a beer
Nothing to fear
It's cold on the street
Nothing guaranteed to eat
So stumble to the bin
Is it actually a sin
To consume the unwanted?
Hiding a face that's haunted
Habits that gnaw away
Leading you astray
Down that grimy path

When did you last have a bath?
Dens to hide the shame
Still injecting your mate who's lame
When will the madness cease
Probably when you're granted a lease
On your own place
A safe space
Away from all the corruption
Cause an eruption
In the house of lords
Get out of the addiction wards

Technology

Everything is digital
There are those who are cynical
Of putting everything on a cloud
They'll be proud
Of sticking to the "good ol' days"
Don't want to change their ways
Sticking with paper and pen
Takes time especially when
In seconds on a phone
You could be applying for a loan
To cover the cost of a new one
This one's torch is as bright as the sun
Until 2 months later
When there'll be a few even greater
Impossible to keep up
Taking cute photos of your pup
To throw across social media
Apps developed making people greedier
Hungry for those thumbs and hearts
Tits more popular than the arts
Strive for years to perfect a talent
Then all these men who act gallant
Gawp over a braless teenager
Its an easy wager
Which one gets you more cash

To go out on the lash
And brag about crypto currency
Or what's trending currently
It's not all bad though
There are seeds to sow
Get a presence established
And soon you'll be lavished
With praise and support
Just mind someone doesn't hit report
A sensitive soul may be offended
And your page might get ended
By the powers at be
Who don't want the world to see
An alternate view
Portrayed by the select few
Media sources
Who'll use all their resources
To cancel a page
Trying to lead us into a new age
Remember it's not real life
So don't let it cause you strife!

Ink

Started off for sailors and whores
In japan it was behind closed doors
Now they're worn with pride
Adding a bounce to many a stride
Black and grey or full of colour
As they age, they get duller
They've grown into an art
And you can't stop once you start
From devils to flowers
In that chair you'll spend hours
Of course they hurt
From your eyes, tears may squirt
From either pain or joy
Your parents they are sure to annoy
So wear them loud
And wear them proud
Show them off whenever you can
Just beware of getting a tan!

Control

Give up your control to me
And I'll let you see
A whole new world of pleasure and pain
There is much for you to gain
On your knees eyes down
You'll be scared to make me frown
See the whips and floggers?
I'll be using them in joggers
Bare skin going red
Did you pay attention to what was said?
The sadistic smile
I'll leave you tied up for a while
Begging and panting
"thank you sir" you'll be chanting
That release I'll finally allow
Sweat running from your brow
Twitching and sagging
To your friends you'll go bragging
About the way we play
Not much will I say
You'll learn the cues
And you will let me use
 The control for good
Some of the tools are made of wood
Not your favourite thing

But when it hits it sings
A beautiful sound
Does make you howl like a hound
But the aftercare
Is always there
Ensuring your comfy and cosy
By the end you're awfully dozy

Christmas Party

Stay at home it's not safe
But we'll rub elbows until they chafe
Thanks for the spending money
How we've found it frightfully funny
That the country was locked away
So in downing street we'll stay
Champagne and caviar
Carry on how you are
The virus will soon be gone
And the laws will be drawn
To protect the wealthy
No longer trying to be stealthy
Might as well bend over
 Why not expense your range rover
Buy a second flat
And rent it out like a dirty rat
People lost a loved one
Yet it was just a bit of fun
For Boris and his crew
About time we organised a coup
But them in the bin
We cannot forgive their sin
Rise up against this farcical behaviour
We must be our own saviour

Deep Breath

In.
Out.
Calm.
Ignore the buzzing in your brain.
Focus on your surroundings.
The floor beneath your feet.
The clouds in the sky.
Zone out from the noise.
In.
Out.
Calm.
Feel the sun on your face.
Rest those jigging legs.
The stormy sea inside your mind
Make a reflective pool of water.
In.
Out.
Calm.
Feel the pressure off your shoulder.
Release the tension in your brow.
Relax your jaw.
In.
Out.
Calm.
Open your eyes.

It's a beautiful day.
In.
Out.
Calm.
And you're back

Blurry Eyed

Blurry eyed
The alarm goes off
Grumbling
Reaching over
Silence
It can't be that time already
Time to work
Time lost
Time poorly spent
Earning money for those precious moments
Spent outside your cage
Your "free" time
But is it?
Put on your suit
Don your overalls
Grab your caffeine
Stumble out your door
This is the life?
9 hours later
Stumble back through the door
Collapse on the sofa
"Dinner's Ready!"

Plonked on your lap
Already falling asleep
Time for bed

Blurry eyed
The alarm goes off....